ESERIES STARWARS
Ne~~~~~~~, ~~~~~~, ~thor.

REBEL POWER!

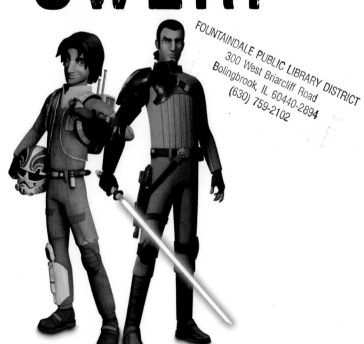

Written by Lauren Nesworthy

Editors Lauren Nesworthy, Anant Sagar
Art Editor Dimple Vohra
Assistant Art Editor Akansha Jain
Senior Art Editor Clive Savage
DTP Designer Umesh Singh Rawat
Pre-Production Producer Marc Staples
Pre-Production Manager Sunil Sharma
Producer David Appleyard
Managing Editors Sadie Smith,
Chitra Subramanyam
Managing Art Editors Neha Ahuja,
Ron Stobbart
Art Director Lisa Lanzarini
Publisher Julie Ferris
Publishing Director Simon Beecroft

Reading Consultant Linda B. Gambrell, Ph.D

For Lucasfilm
Executive Editor Jonathan W. Rinzler
Art Director Troy Alders
Story Group Rayne Roberts, Pablo Hidalgo, Leland Chee

First American Edition, 2015
Published in the United States by DK Publishing
345 Hudson Street, New York, New York 10014

Copyright © 2015 Dorling Kindersley Limited
A Penguin Random House Company
15 16 17 18 19 10 9 8 7 6 5 4 3 2 1
001–279686–July/2015

© & TM 2015 LUCASFILM LTD.

A catalog record for this book is available from the Library of Congress.

ISBN: 978-1-4654-3595-8 (Hardback)
ISBN: 978-1-4654-3596-5 (Paperback)

DK books are available at special discounts when purchased in bulk for sales promotions, premiums, fund-raising, or educational use. For details, contact: DK Publishing Special Markets, 345 Hudson Street, New York, New York 10014
SpecialSales@dk.com

Printed and bound in China

A WORLD OF IDEAS:
SEE ALL THERE IS TO KNOW

www.starwars.com
www.dk.com

Contents

Fighting for Lothal

Since the Empire took over the
galaxy, things have been hard for
the citizens of the planet Lothal.

But a brave group of rebels
is fighting back against the
Imperial army. This is bringing
hope to the people!

Ezra's Album

I look pretty good in my uniform. →

Check out this graffiti in my room. Sabine made it just for me.

Shh... My Master is meditating.

Hera the super pilot! She can outfly any TIE.

Haha! Zeb stinks so bad.

Chopper...?! You ruined my lunch.

Force Training

The Jedi Kanan believes
that the Force is strong
with young Ezra.
Between missions,
Kanan teaches Ezra
how to use his powers.
He shows him what it
truly means to be a Jedi.

HOW TO BECOME A JEDI

A step-by-step GUIDE

Focus is important to master the Force.

Learn new skills like the Force pull, Force jump, and Force push.

The Force enables you to communicate with many kinds of animals.

Prove you are worthy by going through the tough trials. The trials are a test of skill, strength, and wisdom.

Pass the tests to obtain a special crystal and make your own lightsaber.

You are now on your way to becoming a Jedi Knight.

Rebel Attack

The rebels are always
finding ways to ruin things
for the Empire.

The celebrations on Empire Day grind to a halt when Sabine's amazing explosions destroy a brand-new TIE fighter!

REBEL SKILLS

The rebels are armed with a variety of skills.
They use these abilities as they fight the Empire.

Sabine is a weapons expert. Her specialty is making explosives.

SABINE

Hera pilots the *Ghost*. She can outfly the best Imperial pilots.

HERA

Ezra is a Padawan. He is training to become a Jedi Knight.

EZRA

Zeb is a strong warrior. He loves to fight against stormtroopers.

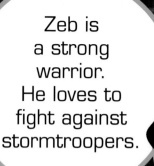

ZEB

KANAN

Kanan is a Jedi. He leads the rebels in their fight against the Empire.

Chopper is a great mechanic. He keeps the *Ghost* in superb shape.

CHOPPER

15

Imperial Influence

The Imperials try to make people believe that being ruled by the Empire is a good thing. They do this by using posters and Holonews messages. This helps the Empire keep everyone under their control.

BE A GOOD CITIZEN

**PEOPLE OF LOTHAL!
YOU ARE ALL
PROUD MEMBERS
OF THE EMPIRE.**

**Remember that
the Empire will only do
what is good for you.**

HERE IS HOW YOU CAN HELP

Obey the Empire's instructions.

Help us track down traitors.

Report all criminals to the nearest Imperial officer.

Support the Empire and its soldiers.

Always celebrate Empire Day.

- By order of
Agent Kallus

Ezra Undercover

Fighting isn't always the best
way to stop the Empire.
Sometimes the rebels have
to be sneaky.
Ezra pretends to be a stormtrooper
cadet at the Imperial Academy.
This gives him a chance to
steal important plans that can
help the rebels.

New Allies

Sometimes new friends can come from unexpected places. Ezra meets two stormtrooper cadets, Zare Leonis and Jai Kell, who help him with his mission at the Academy. The rebels are making more allies!

BECOME A STORMTROOPER

Join the Imperial Academy:
Serve the Empire with pride!

Be part of a team.

Fight against the rebels.

Learn military tactics.

Use deadly weapons.

ALSO, GET AN AWESOME SUIT OF ARMOR!

Stealing Secrets

The Empire may be scary, but that does not stop people from standing up to them.

The rebels rescue a Rodian named Tseebo from the Imperials. He knows many secrets about the Empire, which he shares with the rebels.

Fight the Empire

The rebels know that it's not easy to beat the Empire, but that doesn't stop them from trying. They are always thinking of new ways to succeed.

☑ Help the people of Lothal.

☑ Collect weapons, food, and equipment.

☑ Blow up Imperial property.

☑ Master the use of the Force.

☑ Rescue prisoners from the Empire.

☑ Hack into the communication tower.

☑ Steal Imperial secrets.

☑ Do not get caught by the Empire.

Galactic Businessman

Smuggler Lando Calrissian does not always do the right thing. He has many skills, however, that can help the rebels. A smuggler makes a strong ally against the Empire!

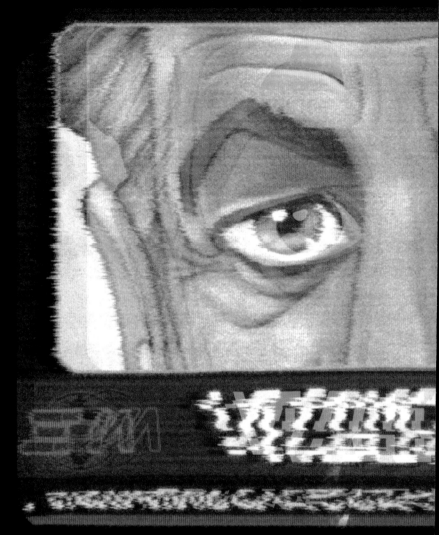

Double Agent

It is hard for the rebels to
know who to trust.
They thought that a man named
Gall Trayvis hated the Empire.

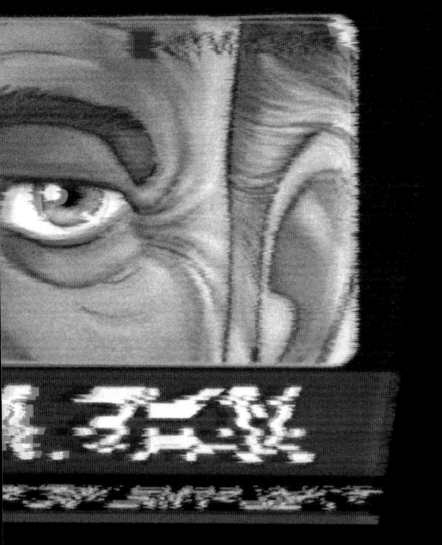

He used broadcasts to speak out
against the Empire and gave the
rebels information using codes.
But he was secretly working for
the Empire all along!

A MESSAGE OF HOPE

The Empire is spreading lies about the rebels. So the rebels are sending out a message to the people of Lothal encouraging them to fight for their freedom.

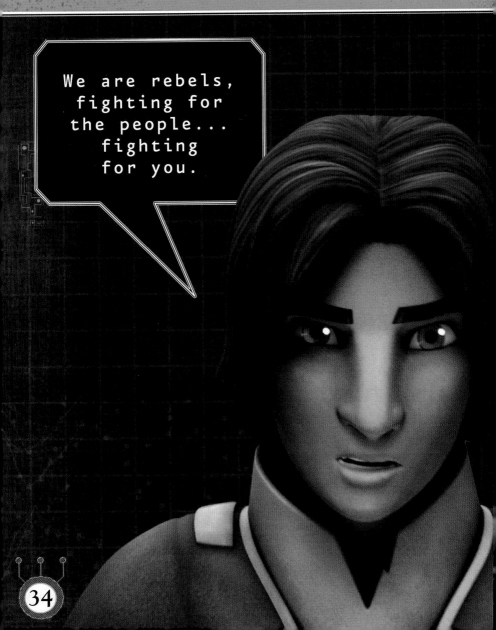

We are rebels, fighting for the people... fighting for you.

...See what the Empire has done to your lives, your families, and your freedom?

It's only gonna get worse... Unless we stand up and fight back...

Stand up, together. Because that's when we're strongest. As one.

Capturing Rebels

No matter how hard the Imperials try to stop the rebels, they are disappointed over and over again! Imperial Governor Grand Moff Tarkin will punish anyone who fails to defeat the rebels.

The Dark Lord

The rebels are growing stronger every day! The Imperials are afraid that more people will join them in the fight against the Empire. Only one man is powerful enough to stop the rebels once and for all... Darth Vader.

Quiz

1. Who is teaching Ezra how to use his powers?

2. What do you get if you pass the Jedi Trials?

3. What does Sabine's explosion destroy on Empire Day?

4. Who is a great mechanic?

5. Who were Ezra's friends at the Imperial Academy?

6. Who is the Rodian that the rebels rescue from the Empire?

7. What is Lando's job?

8. Who is a double agent?

9. Who is the Imperial Governor?

10. Who is powerful enough to stop the rebels?

Answers on page 45

Glossary

Meditating
Thinking calmly.

Undercover
Working in a secret way to collect information.

Tactics
A plan for achieving a goal.

Smuggler
Someone who transports things secretly.

Double agent
Someone who pretends to work for one person, when they are actually working for someone else.

Specialty
Something that a person is particularly good at.

Distraction
Something that makes it hard to pay attention.

Padawan
Someone who is training to become a Jedi.

Index

Answers to the quiz on pages 42 and 43:
1. Kanan 2. A special crystal 3. TIE fighter 4. Chopper
5. Zare Leonis and Jai Kell 6. Tseebo 7. Smuggler
8. Gall Trayvis 9. Grand Moff Tarkin 10. Darth Vader

Guide for Parents

DK Readers is a multi-level interactive reading adventure series for children, developing the habit of reading widely for both pleasure and information. These books have an exciting main narrative interspersed with a range of reading genres to suit your child's reading ability, as required by the Common Core State Standards. Each book is designed to develop your child's reading skills, fluency, grammar awareness, and comprehension in order to build confidence and engagement when reading.

Ready for a *Beginning to Read* book
YOUR CHILD SHOULD

- be able to read many words without needing to stop and break them down into sound parts.
- read smoothly, in phrases and with expression. By this level, your child will be beginning to read silently.
- self-correct when some word or sentence doesn't sound right.

A Valuable and Shared Reading Experience

For some children, text reading, particularly non-fiction, requires much effort, but adult participation can make this both fun and easier. So here are a few tips on how to use this book with your child.

TIP 1 Check out the contents together before your child begins:

- invite your child to check the blurb, contents page, and layout of the book and comment on it.
- ask your child to make predictions about the story.
- talk about the information your child might want to find out.

TIP 2 Encourage fluent and flexible reading:

- support your child to read in fluent, expressive phrases, making full use of punctuation and thinking about the meaning.

- help your child learn to read with expression by choosing a sentence to read aloud and demonstrating how to do this.

TIP 3 Indicators that your child is reading for meaning:

- your child will be responding to the text if he/she is self-correcting and varying his/her voice.
- your child will want to talk about what he/she is reading or is eager to turn the page to find out what will happen next.

TIP 4 Chat at the end of each chapter:

- encourage your child to recall specific details after each chapter.
- let your child pick out interesting words and discuss what they mean.
- talk about what each of you found most interesting or most important.
- ask questions about the text. These help to develop comprehension skills and awareness of the language used.

A FEW ADDITIONAL TIPS

- Read to your child regularly to demonstrate fluency, phrasing, and expression; to find out or check information; and for sharing enjoyment.
- Encourage your child to reread favorite texts to increase reading confidence and fluency.
- Check that your child is reading a range of different types of material, such as poems, jokes, and following instructions.

Series consultant, **Dr. Linda Gambrell**, Distinguished Professor of Education at Clemson University, has served as President of the National Reading Conference, the College Reading Association, and the International Reading Association. She is also reading consultant for the **DK Adventures.**

Have you read these other great books from DK?

BEGINNING TO READ ALONE

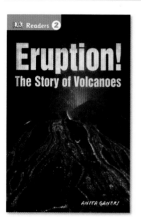

What spits out fire and ash? Find out all about volcanoes.

Meet a band of rebels, brave enough to take on the Empire!

The Inquisitor is coming. Now there is no safe place for the Jedi to hide!

READING ALONE

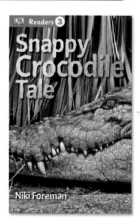

Join the heroes of the rebellion as they continue to fight the Empire.

Learn all about Yoda's battles and how he uses the Force.

Follow Chris Croc's adventures from a baby to a mighty king.